# ~ THE ~
# SHAMELESS
# LIAR'S
# GUIDE

D1365041

## BY DUKE CHRISTOFFERSEN

SOURCEBOOKS HYSTERIA™
AN IMPRINT OF SOURCEBOOKS, INC.®
NAPERVILLE, ILLINOIS

Published by Sourcebooks, Inc.
P.O. Box 4410, Naperville, Illinois 60567-4410
(630) 961-3900
FAX: (630) 961-2168
www.sourcebooks.com

ISBN 13: 978-1-4022-0509-5

Library of Congress Cataloging-in-Publication Data

Christoffersen, Duke
  The shameless liar's guide / Duke Christoffersen.
     p. cm.
 ISBN 1-4022-0509-0 (alk. paper)
 1. Truthfulness and falsehood—Humor. I. Title.

PN6231.T74C47 2005
81'.607—dc22
2005020142

Printed and bound in the United States of America.
VP   10  9  8  7  6  5  4  3  2  1

Everything you will read in
this book is true...honest.

Dedicated to all the people who believe the crap that comes out of my mouth.

# Table of Contents

# Acknowledgments

I want to express the utmost gratitude to all those people who believed in me, even though I was probably lying to them. Deb, that means you. Thanks for giving me the chance.

I want to express the ut-utmost gratitude to my family. Thanks to Valba, Kevin, Libba, and Jenny for teaching me how to lie. And big thanks to Chris and Beth (my parents) for threatening to punish me if I lied. Fear is a great motivator for not getting caught.

I'd also like to throw some gratitude to the other liars that I call my friends, specifically the Frost for being there, and to Ballard for not being there when I needed a place to crash.

Jeanette and Rick know I am grateful for their help. I don't lie to them...or do I?

I have to offer gratitude to my ex-wife…if both of you are reading this, you can both believe I'm talking about you. No matter which, I never lied to either of you (about anything major anyway). I never needed to.

And eternal love and gratitude to Cornbread, my ex-dog, the only little guy who always knew when I was lying. Dogs can sense that, you know.

# Introduction

> "It is always the best policy to speak
> the truth—unless, of course, you are
> an exceptionally good liar."
>
> **—Jerome K. Jerome**

The journey on which you are about to embark will transform you from an ordinary person who lies into an extraordinary liar, and every journey begins with one step…except this one. It begins with two:

**Step 1:** You must accept the truth, and the truth is that you lie.

**Step 2:** You must *stop* accepting your inability to lie well.

If you say that you don't lie or that you're going to stop lying, then you're off to a good start, because you're only lying to yourself (which will be covered later).

Everyone lies. If this is true (which it is), then why are so few people good at it? There are many reasons that people are bad liars. First, they have been raised to believe that lying is bad. That's not true. Lying isn't bad; *bad* lying is bad. Second, we live in a world with billions of people who lie and get caught. The more people we have, the more people get caught, and the more people get caught, the more skeptical people we have who don't believe what you're saying even before you open your mouth. Third, rapid technological advancement makes it difficult for you to lie. The mass communication and recording devices we have today trip up liars in ways that were impossible as few as a hundred years ago. And last and most important, no one has ever taught you how to lie well.

By the time you finish this book, you will be able to overcome all the obstacles that face the modern liar. You will understand that lying is not bad, but necessary for survival. You will overcome the skeptics by learning how to establish trust. You will learn how to use (and not use) technology in ways that will keep you from getting caught. And, if you follow the ABCDE's of Lying, and strictly obey the 10 Lying Laws, you will have the skills necessary to transform you from someone who once felt bad about lying into someone who is not only good at it, but someone who has turned it into an art form.

**Enjoy the journey.**

# *Chapter 1*

## What Would Your Life Be Like If You Didn't Lie?

> "An injurious lie is an uncommend-
> able thing; and so, also, and in the
> same degree, is an injurious truth."
> —Mark Twain

What would your life be like if you didn't lie? It would be short and lonely.

If you never lied, you would lack the basic survival necessities and you would alienate all the people who would otherwise be a support system for you. You would ultimately die of starvation, exposure, sleep deprivation, or some combination of the three. And you would die alone.

At first, everything would be fine. Your family, friends, coworkers, and employers would appreciate your honesty. But slowly, you would find that when you tell people things like, "Hey, Bob, your hair looks a lot thinner than it did a couple months ago; you're going to be completely bald by the time you're thirty-five. It's too bad your chances of finding a life partner are getting as thin as your hair," they want absolutely nothing to do with you.

Face it, the truth actually *does* hurt, and nobody wants to be around someone who hurts them. It starts when you tell your coworkers things that they don't want to hear and they go complain to your boss. You'd think your boss would defend you because you're a hard worker, but that's not true. Nobody works hard enough to satisfy their boss—they pretend to work hard and lie about how busy they are, so they don't get more work piled on them. Not you, though. You tell your boss that you get bored before lunch and start playing minesweeper or solitaire. That would probably be okay, except you also tell him that he needs to lose about twenty pounds or the wife that's too good for him is going to leave him for the young, good-looking intern in the mail room that she's probably sleeping with anyway.

Now you're out of a job…or maybe you've done this before and you're out of two or three jobs, but that's unlikely, because after the first couple of times, you have no real professional references. So, you use your friends as references on your résumé. You could ask them to lie for you and tell your prospective employer that they are former employers or coworkers, but that's lying by proxy, also unacceptable to you.

Even if you wanted to ask your friends to lie for you, it wouldn't matter because you've made the mistake of being honest with them, too: "Amy, did you ever consider the fact that the men you're interested in are way out of your league? I mean, if you were as attractive as you think you are, then maybe not, but have you looked in the mirror since high school?"

So now you can't get any job at all and you go to your friends to borrow some money to get you by until you get back on your feet, but…oh wait, you don't have anymore friends. That's okay, you have parents who will bail you out. Mom and Dad are always there when you need them. Ironically, the very people who told you lying is wrong have disowned you because you told them: "I think you both did a half-ass parenting job and everything that's wrong with me is your fault. If you hadn't screamed at each other and gotten divorced when I was eleven, I wouldn't be a dysfunctional mass of emotional and psychological issues."

You have no job, which means you have no money of your own. You have no friends or family from whom you can borrow the money. You can't beg for money on the street because when you tell the strangers from whom you're begging that you're not going to use the money to buy a bottle of cheap wine, they'll think you're lying.

You have no food. You don't even have water to drink because you have to buy that now, too. You're hungry, thirsty, broke, and alone, but that's okay because you sleep well at night knowing that you are a totally honest person.

Only you're not sleeping too well at night, because you're sleeping on a park bench or under an overpass, and no amount of newsprint or honesty is going to keep you warm. You might wake up every morning and say, "It's okay that I'm starving, cold, and thirsty, because I'm an honest person and I never lie." Do you know who you'd be saying that to? You'd be saying that to yourself, or a sporting good that you drew a face on and named.

You've hit rock bottom. You're thinking about lying, but instead you decide you're going to have to find some food, shelter, water, and a place to sleep without doing that. So you break into someone's house, steal their food, drink their water, and sleep in their bed. The cops show up and ask you what you're doing there. Then, instead of telling them that you're an exterminator, a TV repairman, or a building inspector, you tell them truth: "I broke in to steal their food, drink their water, and sleep in their bed." The police don't care that you're honest; they care that you broke the law.

You're admittedly guilty of breaking and entering *and* burglary. You're down at the police station and you have one phone call. You can't call friends or family, because you have no friends and your family won't help you. You could call an attorney, but no attorney is going to help you because you have no money. You're stuck with the public defender, only he's the public defender because he graduated from the bottom of his law school class. Why? Because he can't lie worth a damn either. You're screwed. You're going to the state pen for two to five for committing two felony offenses, when all you had to do in the first place is lie...it's not even a crime.

Oh yeah, and the other basic need you'll lack—sex. In prison you'll be able to get some, but probably not the kind you want. And when you get out, I can assure you that nobody is going to have sex with someone who doesn't have a home, a job, friends, or family, and just did time in the state pen. Nobody...unless you tell them you have a nice car or a stockpile of cash. But you won't do that; you don't lie.

# Chapter 2

## The History of Lying

**"The history of our race, and each individual's experience, are sown thick with evidence that a truth is not hard to kill and that a lie told well is immortal."**

**—Mark Twain**

Lying is immortal, but not immoral. It never has been, and it never will be. It is necessary for survival. Lying is directly responsible for the survival of our species. People have been doing it since the beginning of time. It is older than fire, the wheel, and even the club (the blunt object, not the anti-theft device). Actual lies are inventions, but the need to lie is as innate as the need for food, love, and a piping hot cup of coffee first thing in the morning.

The very first people were faced with two options: death or deception. They wisely chose deception. Because they did, they flourished and populated the earth with more liars. Those liars begat more liars who begat more liars and so on, and now we are members of a world population of several billion liars.

The only difference between now and the beginning of time is that the modern liar faces a lot more challenges than our predecessors. Of course, our lives are much easier than the lives of our primitive ancestors— they didn't have microwave ovens or instant oatmeal. However, if we time-warped some Neanderthal to the twenty-first century, he might eat like a king, but he wouldn't be able to lie worth a damn. People are much more skeptical than they used to be, and there are billions of them. Not to mention that the more technology we have, the more difficult it is to lie and get away with it.

However, if you are an American, you have a head start on the rest of the world. You come from a long history of liars. Early Americans were not artful about their lies, but they got what they wanted from them (i.e., a brand new, big country).

But you don't have to be an American to be a liar. Lying doesn't discriminate. Regardless of your religion, color, gender, sexual orientation, or mental state, you are a liar. And if you want to be an artful liar, you can't go forward until you know where you've been.

# The Dawn of Deception

**"An omnipotent God is the only being with no reason to lie."**

**—Mason Cooley**

As I alluded to earlier, humans are alive on this planet for one reason: the first people learned early that they needed to deceive in order to prosper. They needed deception in order to eat. They needed deception in order to procreate. Those who did not understand this, or lacked the ability to deceive, perished.

One might argue that the first people didn't need to deceive; they only needed to learn how to hunt, gather, create fire, find shelter, etc. That's true, except that they could not do these things successfully until they first discovered how to deceive (I use the word "deceive" because people who can only grunt, point, and draw crude stick pictures on cave walls cannot technically "lie;" that requires speaking).

I'm not saying that Cro-Magnon and Neanderthal people sat around in a cave telling each other lies and that's the reason we are here today. I'm saying that they learned very quickly that without deception, they would die. The only difference between their primordial deception and our modern lying is that, when they deceived, they didn't feel the least bit guilty and they certainly weren't afraid of getting caught. They were afraid of not having something to eat, having nowhere warm to sleep at night, and not living to see their 20th birthday. How did they allay these fears? They deceived.

Only after learning how to deceive could the first people survive long enough to sustain their health, and, in turn, live long enough to discover fire, agriculture, and the other basic technologies that perpetuated our race. Once they had health, time, and energy, they could procreate…except they realized that they also needed to deceive in order to do that.

Getting two cave people together in a situation conducive to lovemaking would have been impossible without deception. First, they had no privacy because they didn't have rooms—they all lived together in one cave. Second, the caveman couldn't woo his cavewoman with a candlelight dinner—he didn't have fire. Third, if you've seen pictures, you know these cave people weren't very attractive, and I don't know for sure, but I don't think they probably smelled too good. So the caveman had to deceive his cavewoman in order to get her to make love to him. He waited until it got dark, hid behind a rock with his club in hand, and waited for the cavewoman to emerge. Not only did this technique work, but it spawned two phrases that are still in use today: "night club," a place where men lie in order to have sex, and "Not tonight, honey. I have a headache."

Just as the caveman deceived in order to have sex, the cavewoman learned early that if she wanted the miserable, but necessary, experience to terminate quickly, she had to deceive, too. This is the origin of a practice that is still in common use today: the faking of the orgasm.

Because both caveman and cavewoman learned to lie, the species flourished. Before too long, people were walking upright, cooking their food, brushing, flossing, and inventing more things that made their existence more comfortable and fruitful.

If you think that lying wasn't, or still isn't, necessary for survival, or if you still think that lying is immoral, read the following fable—there's a moral.

A tribe of cavemen were hanging out with the cavewomen and they got hungry, so they went outside to find some berries or some roots. They found quite a few, but the ones that didn't make them sick or kill them weren't enough to sustain them, so the cavewomen insisted that the cavemen go out and kill some large prehistoric animals while the cavewomen collected the good roots and berries. The cavemen were less than ecstatic about the idea, but they needed more food, and necessity can make you do things that—no matter how small and Neanderthal your brain is—you are compelled to do. So the cavemen left their cave and went out to hunt without the benefit of weapons. One hungry, brave/stupid caveman saw a saber-toothed tiger in a clearing. He walked right up to the giant beast and promptly proceeded to attempt to kill him with nothing more than his bare, hairy hands. That caveman was swiftly devoured by the big cat. His more cowardly/intelligent cohorts crouched behind the bushes and watched in horror as their cave mate ironically became the meal of the animal he meant to eat.

The cavemen returned to the cave empty-handed, knowing they had to do something different from their deceased companion. They went back to the drawing wall and brainstormed a variety of cat-killing options. They came to the conclusion that they could not kill him with their hands: they needed a weapon to combat the tiger's saber teeth and claws. They put their heads together and came up with what we now know as a club.

Feeling good about their new idea, the braver (and now smaller) group went out to face the tiger. One of the remaining cavemen went up to the saber-toothed tiger armed with his new state-of-the-art weapon. He approached the beast and was promptly devoured in the same brutal fashion as his predecessor.

Luckily, one of the smarter cavemen saw this and thought, "The club was a good idea. The bad idea was letting the tiger see him…and eat him." So he had an idea: "I'm going to hunt the tiger with my club, only I'm not going to face the tiger. I'm going to climb a tree and wait for him to walk beneath me. When he does, I'll drop from the tree, surprising him with a vicious blow to the head. Then we'll have a feast."

His friends sat in the tree and watched him descend on the cat, surprising him with a vicious blow. The cat went down. The others realized that the weapon was not what was going to feed them, but it was the deception that was going to fill their stomachs. They happily dragged the carcass back to the cave to a more-than-warm welcome from the women.

They feasted for hours. After their feast, the women were happy. They recognized that their men fed them and extended their short lives for an extra couple of weeks. The women were happy to repay them for their efforts. So the heroes, thanks to the deception of one crafty caveman, got to make love to all of the cavewomen.

Everything was perfect and some of the women were with child, but the food was running out and the men needed to go back out and hunt again. They were fine with this because they knew how to deceptively lure the animals into a place where they could hunt and kill them successfully.

This went okay for a while, until the animals, who at the time were about as smart as the humans, figured out what these guys were up to. The club in the tree thing stopped working and the whole system almost fell apart.

Then one day, a cowardly caveman told the other hunters that he would stay behind at the cave while the others hunted and come up with some more innovative ways to hunt, so that they didn't have to work as hard at what they did. They reluctantly agreed. The cowardly caveman went to the drawing wall and came up with something that would kill the beast from a distance, keeping the hunters as far as possible out of harm's way.

When his cave mates came back one day empty-handed from a hunt, they asked him if he had come up with anything new that would make their lives easier. He showed them the spear. They all oohhed and ahhhed and excitedly took their new weapons out for the hunt. They asked the inventor if he wanted to go. He shook his big head and motioned that he was going to stay behind and invent newer and better weapons. They didn't mind this, because he was doing good work. However, he was satisfied with the spear and relished the fact that he was the only man in a cave full of women.

The women, realizing that the spear this man had invented would bring them more food, lavished him with attention—so much so that he stopped coming up with new ways to hunt.

This was great for him for a while, but soon the women lost respect for him because he was lazy and no longer contributing to their survival. So the coward figured, if he was going to be able to stay in the cave and stay in the favor of the women, he would have to come up with a newer, better weapon. He racked his tiny brain and soon came to the conclusion that the spear was the best he was going to do. He was going to have to go out and hunt. Hunting, spear or no spear, was not an option for this coward, so he came up with a way to keep from doing this: "I'll just tell them that I have a new weapon that I'm working on, but it's not finished yet. Give me some time." Based on his success with the spear, the hunters happily accepted his story. The women, however, knew better because they were there and because, of course, even cavewomen know when men are lying to them.

He didn't have to hunt, but his days of philandering with the women were over. He realized that he had to remedy this immediately. He tried some gentle but transparent attempts at seduction, but the women saw through these lame attempts immediately.

Desperate, he thought for a while and came to the following conclusion: "I'll hunt a woman the same way we hunt the tiger—I'll trick her into making love with me." I can't throw a spear at her, because that will kill her, and I can't bang her over the head with a club because that will also...wait a second...if I hit her on the head with a club, but not as hard as I would hit a tiger, it will stun her just enough that I'll be able to make love to her.

So one night, while the men were on a hunt, the coward placed some fresh berries outside the cave and hid behind a rock, club in hand. Sure enough, a hungry woman saw the berries, emerged from the cave and was surprised by a knock on the head.

Unfortunately for the caveman, this technique didn't work very long. The other women became wise to his brutality and eventually he had to either go out and hunt with the others or come up with better weapons.

Because the spear was the best he could do, he was forced to hunt. Spear in his sweaty, nervous hand, he crouched in the grass, looking for a tiger, but he didn't realize that a tiger was crouching in the grass, looking for him. Before he knew what happened the tiger pounced on him and ate him.

**The Moral:** Deceiving is necessary for survival, but you have to continue to get better at it or you will die in the jaws of a giant prehistoric cat...figuratively speaking, of course.

**Disclaimer:** Head clubbing, however effective a million years ago, is no longer acceptable in modern society.

# Technology, Population, and Lying

In the twenty-first century, we have more luxuries than our ancestors had, but we don't have the luxury of lying and being confident that we won't get caught. Liars today have the challenge of overcoming obstacles that past liars did not have to overcome, and those obstacles are getting larger and more plentiful every day. Several billion people live on the earth, and those people have technology at their disposal that makes it exceedingly difficult to lie and not get caught. Consequently, as more people inhabit the earth, and more people get caught, more people have become skeptical—they think they're being lied to before the alleged liar has ever opened his mouth.

Notice the following line graph:

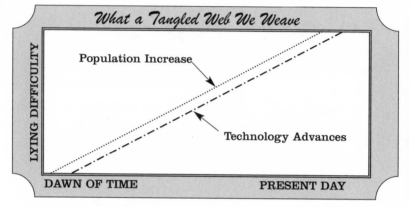

*What a Tangled Web We Weave*

**LYING DIFFICULTY**

Population Increase

Technology Advances

**DAWN OF TIME**          **PRESENT DAY**

*As time passes, those who weave the webs are more likely to get caught in their own webs.*

A million years ago, only a hundred or so people roamed the earth. They didn't have any form of mass communication or documentation—they didn't have a written language, much less anything to write it on. Besides, if only a hundred people exist, there are fewer people who have to believe the lie.

A thousand years ago, things weren't that much different than a million years ago. Sure, there were a hell of a lot more people, but they all lived in villages that were several days away from other villages on horseback or camelback. They had a written language, and the means to document things, but if you lied about something that was written down, you could steal the scroll or parchment it was written on, burn it, and feel pretty confident that the feudal lord or chief in your village didn't have your documented lie backed up on floppy disk.

As little as 150 years ago, lying was relatively simple compared to today. People in the mid-nineteenth century corresponded either via letter or face-to-face. Nobody in Civil War time ever accidentally hit the call button on their cell phone when they were gossiping about the person they just dialed. Nobody in the roaring twenties ever had more than one Instant Messaging (IM) screen up and typed a message to the wrong person. A cowboy in the old west who didn't have a telephone, much less caller ID, couldn't start to call his wife from the saloon, but hang up real fast because he realized she would track the number and know he wasn't helping someone build a barn like he said he was doing.

The cowboy's life might have been more difficult than our lives today. He had to go the dentist without the benefit of happy gas or soothing music. He had to sleep on dirt next to a horse, and he didn't have TiVo. However, he could lie and not get caught because he didn't have email, IM, a cell phone with a camera on it, a Palm Pilot, caller ID, three-way calling, or a nosy neighbor with a handheld video camera and a lot of time on her hands.



In a nutshell, if you're going to be an artful liar in the twenty-first century, you have to be better than ever before. You have to be ever-mindful of the pitfalls that are waiting to trip you up.

A few ways to avoid being tripped up by technology:

* Don't IM more than one person at the same time. You might accidentally type the wrong thing in the wrong field, and once you send that message, it's not coming back.

❊ Don't ever *ever* use three-way calling or confer-
ence calling, unless you know for a fact that
you aren't going to lie. You might think that the
person you're now talking about has clicked off,
but you never know for sure...until they tell you
they heard what you said.

❊ Don't trust your auto key lock function on your
cell phone. My friend called his girlfriend from
Vegas and he didn't mean to call his girlfriend
from Vegas. Enough said.

❊ Don't write emails that contain lies unless
you're pretty damn sure you can remember
exactly what you wrote. Strike that—don't lie
via email. Period.

❊ Don't record any lies on audio or video for pos-
terity's sake or to remember what you said so
that you can cover your lie. I call this the
"Watergate Principle."

* Don't call someone and tell them you're somewhere you're not. You can never be sure how that number shows up on the caller ID.

* Don't lie to someone about information they can quickly look up on the Internet. Assume they know how to Google something.

* Don't lie about anything that was photographed or videotaped. A picture tells a thousand words, and there's a really good chance they're not going to be the same words you said.

## America—The Melting Pot of Liars

Just as Australia is a country descended from criminals, America is a country descended from liars. They weren't necessarily artful liars, because they got caught, but lying did get the first Americans what they wanted: a huge piece of land.

America was founded on lying. Columbus told the natives that he was their friend. The Puritans told the king they were just going for a little boat ride—they'd be right back. Settlers told the Native Americans that they were just visiting. Liars from all over the world needed a land where they could lie freely. They heard that in America we had this thing called "freedom of speech." When they realized that you could say anything you want, true or not, they got on a boat and spirited straight to Ellis Island and moved right on in.

Now, after four hundred years of lying, America is the most powerful country in the world. Because we're better than everyone else? Nope. Because we're better liars than everyone else.

The following timeline illustrates some of the more monumental lies in American history. Note that, although effective, these lies are not necessarily artful. The people who told them may have gotten what they wanted from the lie, but they also got caught. You're going to learn to tell great lies and not get caught.

## A Brief History of Lying in America

**1492** — Columbus comes over and tells the natives that everything is cool; they just want to hang out for a little while. The lie was not successful because the natives believed him; the lie was successful because when Columbus delivered it, he breathed some small pox germs on the natives.

**1620** — The Pilgrims tell Squanto and the other Native Americans with whom they share the first Thanksgiving, "We're not going to slaughter you and take all your stuff after you feed us." They almost pulled off a great lie, until they started slaughtering and taking all the stuff.

**17-hundred-something** — George Washington makes up a story about how he confessed to cutting down a cherry tree that he never cut down. He lied to make people believe he was honest. Innovative and brilliant, but he still got caught. However...who's on the one dollar bill and the quarter now?

**1804** — Modern day Missouri — Lewis tells a tired, hungry Clark: "We're almost there." The lie convinced Clark to keep helping Lewis, but Clark eventually realized Lewis was lying somewhere near the Montana/ South Dakota border.

**1860** — Lincoln names himself "Honest Abe" and then pretends like someone else gave him that moniker. At the time, brilliant, but now seen as an obvious attempt to curry favor with the voters. Still, we have to give him credit—he freed the slaves and has his picture on the five dollar bill and the penny.

**1876** — Little Bighorn Battlefield — General George Armstrong Custer tells troops, "Don't worry. Everything's going to be fine." The men stayed and fought with him, but this one doesn't count because Custer didn't know he was lying. He was an arrogant bastard who really thought he was going to win.

**1929** — America's financial advisors tell investors, "Don't worry. Everything's going to be fine." They weren't lying; they were misunderstood. What they meant by "going to be fine" was "going to be fine for us."

**1974** — Nixon proclaims, "I am not a crook." He was forced to resign and was widely known as a crook thereafter. But...he still got all the amazing benefits afforded to our former presidents.

**1999** — Clinton denies, "I did not have sexual relations with that woman." Oh, he got caught all right, but then later admitted his indiscretion and cashed in on the book.

If you are an American, you may have to overcome the urge to tell brutish lies. That's up to you. And if you're not an American, know that you are by no means behind the other starting liars that have their U.S. citizenship. You don't have to be an American to be a great liar.

## The Greatest Liar in the History of the World

41

I have no idea who this is. He never got caught.

After you finish this book, it might be you, but you'll be the only one who knows. And if you're not, go ahead and tell people that you are. They'll probably believe you. If they don't, they won't be able to prove you're lying.

# *Chapter 3*

## Calculate Your F.I.B. (Fabrication Inclination Barometer)

> "Carlyle said, 'A lie cannot live.' It shows that he did not know how to tell them."
>
> **—Mark Twain**

Before you really dig in and start learning the skills you'll need to be an artful liar, you have to first assess your current liar level. To assess your current liar level, we must calculate your Fabrication Inclination Barometer (F.I.B.). Your F.I.B. score is not an indication of how well you lie, but of how *inclined* you are to do so.

Simply answer True or False to the following twenty questions. Don't lie when you answer the questions; you're not ready for that yet. When you finish, tally all of your true answers and multiply that amount by five.

Answer True or False (I trust you will answer honestly.)

T 1. I lie at least once a day.

T 2. I know when to lie and when not to.

T 3. I add details to stories that weren't really there to make my life seem more interesting than it really is.

T 4. Lying is okay.

F 5. I don't feel *at all* guilty when I lie.

T 6. I have lied for selfish reasons, but have rationalized an altruistic motive.

T 7. I have lied to avoid hurting someone's feelings.

T 8. I have lied to a family member.

T 9. I have lied to a friend.

F 10. I have lied to my dog.

F 11. I know when other people are lying.

F 12. I have called in sick when I was fine.

F 13. I have lied to the police.

F 14. I have never lied in a letter/email/voice mail message.

F 15. I have a great memory.

**46**

F 16. O.J. did it.

F 17. Omitting pieces of the truth is still lying.

T 18. Honesty can be a form of lying.

T 19. The truth and reality are different things.

F 20. I have never been caught lying.

**Your F.I.B. score:**

0–20 Fibber

21–40 Truth Stretcher

41–60 Embellisher

61–80 Bald-Faced Liar

81–99 Compulsive Liar

100 Pathological Liar. You lied on the test. You don't need this book. Give it to someone else...and tell them you wrote it.

If you are a fibber, don't lose hope. If you are a compulsive liar, don't think you have it mastered—I'm certain you didn't answer "True" to number twenty.

No matter what you scored on the F.I.B. test, just think of the end of this book as the highest tower in the castle, and when you make it to the top of that tower, you will be an artful liar. No ladder or elevator or escalator can get you to the top—you have to take every stair. But before you can get inside to the stairs, you have to get past the dragon that's guarding the gate. That dragon's name is "Guilt." If you can get past "Guilt," the rest of the steps will be easy. Go forward bravely.

# Chapter 4

## The Pinocchio Effect

**"The mouth may lie, alright, but the face it makes nonetheless tells the truth."**

**—Friedrich Nietzsche**

You are a bad liar right now because you can't get past the guilt. It's not your fault—it's your parents' fault. They told you the worst lie of all: Lying Is Wrong.

Unfortunately, this lie has been passed down successfully through so many generations that it is no longer mere moral mumbo jumbo; it is embedded into the core of your genetic makeup. Just as you share your parents' eye color and their hair color, you share their inability to lie well, because you share their *guilt*.

Every time you lie, you feel guilty, and every time you feel guilty, it shows. That is why you get caught. In a sense, you're just like Pinocchio. Every time he lies, his nose grows. Every time you lie, your guilt shows.

*The Pinocchio Effect:*

*The inability to lie successfully because of tell-tale signs brought on by guilt.*

But there is hope. Just as you can change your eye color with contact lenses and your hair color with hair dye, you will soon be able to not feel or show guilt when you lie.

# *Chapter 5*

## Conscience Preparation

> **"And, after all, what is a lie? 'Tis but the truth in masquerade."**
> **—George Gordon Noel Byron**

Conscience preparation is required to get you warmed up and ready to lie. Don't worry; I'm not going to turn you into some immoral monster. You already lie; I'm just going to help you not feel bad about it.

## *Lying Law #1*
### *The Truth Hurts, but I Don't*

If you feel good about something, it's difficult to feel guilty about it. There's a lot more to removing generations of guilt, but we're going to start slowly with two simple exercises that will help you.

55

**Exercise 1:** Walk up to someone you know and say, "Hey, have you been working out? You look great!"

They may work out all the time, but there's a good chance that they look the same as they did yesterday. All you did was make someone feel better through a simple lie. Feels pretty good, huh?

**Exercise 2:** Repeat the following mantra five times as you take deep breaths. Don't do this in front of other people, because not only will they think you look stupid, they'll know that you are probably going to lie to them in the near future.

*I am a bad liar, not a bad person.*
*I am a bad liar, not a bad person.*
*I am a bad liar, not a bad person.*
*I am a bad liar, not a bad person.*
*I am a bad liar, not a bad person.*

Did that hurt? Nope. But that was just a toe in the water to let you know that the water's fine. So, let's dive right in!

# Chapter 6

## The ABCDE's of Lying

> **"The lie is the basic building block of good manners. That may seem mildly shocking to a moralist—but then what isn't?"**
>
> **—Quentin Crisp**

Every art has its foundation in science. Just as the roots of music are mathematical and the roots of sculpting physical, the art of lying begins with an empirical, step-by-step process that I call the ABCDE's of Lying. They are the foundation of every lie you tell. Once you have mastered your ABCDE's, you will be able to add your own style and flair to the lies you tell. As with any rules that you learn, there will be exceptions to these as well, but to truly master anything, you have to know the rules before you can break them.

**A**ssess the Situation — First, assess whether or not to lie. Honesty is not always the best policy, but sometimes it is.

**B**uild the Lie — Now that you have decided to lie, you must decide what type of lie to tell and you have to craft the details of that lie...and remember every single one of them.

**C**onvince Yourself It's True — This is hands down the most important step to master. You have decided to lie. You know what the lie is (inside and out). Now, you have to convince yourself that it's true.

**D**eliver the Lie — You've committed to lying. You know the lie. You believe the lie to be true. And now all you have to do is actually tell it.

**E**scape the Situation — Very simply, don't hang around and wait for someone to ask any questions.

# *Assess the Situation*

**"Truth does not consist in never lying but in knowing when to lie and when not to do so."**

**—Samuel Butler**

Lying is something that transcends culture, creed, race, religion, sexual orientation, and gender. It is something we all do for exactly the same reasons...with one exception:

Men lie to have sex (e.g., I drive a Porsche).

Women lie to NOT have sex (e.g., I have a headache).

Disregarding the previous anomaly, we all lie for the same reasons, and if you know those reasons, you can *assess* any situation and decide whether or not lying is the right path to take. In most cases, you won't have a lot of time to make that decision, so remember the following four reasons to lie. If you can accomplish any of the following, lie. If not, don't.

The four reasons to lie:
1. To entertain the listener.
2. To avoid hurting someone's feelings.
3. To avoid pain or embarrassment.
4. To establish a false trust that paves the way for future lying.

## Entertain the Listener (a.k.a. Embellishing)

If more exciting things *really* happened throughout our day, we wouldn't have to lie (embellish). But if we want to make it more fun for the listener, then we have to "add a little texture" to our stories.

### *Lying Law #2:*
*Life's More Fun When Tales Are Spun*

### Example:

You just got off a long flight and your girlfriend picks you up at the gate. She wants to know how your flight was. As usual, it was relatively uneventful, but you did have one experience that was less than fun: An obese lady sat in the seat next to you and didn't have the courtesy to recognize that she was taking up a solid one-third of the space that you paid for.

Which is a better way to relay the story to your loved one?

"A heavyset lady sat next to me on my flight home," or "I didn't think anyone would take the seat next to me, until the sweaty fat lady with the walker and the greasy bag of McDonald's rumbled down the aisle, plopped next to me, lifted up the armrest, and overflowed into my lap."

Was she sweating? Did she have a walker or French fries? No, but it's so much more fun for your girlfriend that way...unless your girlfriend is also obese.

## Avoid Hurting Someone's Feelings

**"For my part, if a lie may do thee grace,
I'll gild it with the happiest terms I have."**

**—William Shakespeare**

This form of lying is a result of someone asking you an uncomfortable question, that in most cases, they don't really want to know the answer to. Here are three questions that must be answered when assessing this situation:

**1.** Do I care enough about this person to save their feelings?

If yes, continue to question 2. If the answer to this question is no, tell them the truth.

### Example:

Scott from accounting bugs the hell out of you, but for some reason he thinks you're his buddy. He wants to ask out Jennifer from marketing, but she is way out of his league. Scott asks you if you think he has a shot with Jennifer from marketing. You say, "Scott, you don't have a chance with her. She's way out of your league." The truth just caused Scott a small amount of pain...a pain that will keep him from bugging you in the future.

**2.** Does this person really want the truth or do they want me to tell them what they want to hear?

People inherently know how fat, thin, unattractive, detestable, or untalented, they are, but most of the time, they want to believe the opposite. They just want to hear the best. Even if they are completely delusional, you don't need to be the person to shatter their delusions. Let someone else do it.

**Example:**
Let's take the previous example with Scott from accounting, except now Scott is one of your best friends. Scott asks you if you think he has a shot with Jennifer in marketing. You lie, "Sure, buddy, I think you should ask her out. What do you have to

lose?" Scott's feelings are going to be hurt, but that's going to be Jennifer's job, not yours. You benefit because Scott will still be your friend and he will ultimately learn that he has no chance with Jennifer anyway.

**3.** Will it benefit me more to tell them the truth or to lie?

### Example:

Now Scott is your boss. He wants to ask Jennifer out. A little trickier, huh? Even though Scott is the boss and probably makes a lot more money than when he was just some peon in accounting, he still has no chance with Jennifer in marketing. He asks you if you think he has a chance with Jennifer. Do you lie? Hell yes! Lying here will benefit your career. If you don't lie, you will most likely be seeking employment elsewhere.

*Lying Law #3*
## If You Lie to Succeed, You Succeed in Lying

## Avoid Pain or Embarrassment
**"Lying increases the creative faculties, expands the ego, and lessens the frictions of social contacts."**

**—Clare Booth Luce**

Most of the time that you lie to avoid hurting someone's feelings, you're also avoiding pain. But this time, you could care less about the other person's feelings; you just don't want to face the painful consequences of an honest answer.

### Example:
You are sitting at home doing nothing. An acquaintance whom you like, but has been getting on your nerves lately, calls and asks you to join her in a lame activity that you want no part of. You could say no thanks, but this acquaintance is very persist-

ent. You don't really care about hurting her feelings; you just don't want to have to deal with her whining about you two never hanging out anymore...which is probably one of the reasons you don't want to hang out. Do you lie to this person? Sure you do.

## Establish False Trust to Pave the Way for Future Lying

This is a little more complicated than other scenarios, because you're not lying right away; you're telling a difficult truth so that you can lie in the future. In other words, you're making someone believe that you're always a 100 percent honest when you're not.

This is a very risky proposition because the truth that you tell has to be just dangerous enough to convince the listener that you're always honest. A good time to use this technique is when you first meet someone.

### Example:

You just start dating a new person, and you run into an ex of yours. The new person asks if you still have feelings for the ex. Let's assume that you do. Do you tell the truth? Absolutely. Your candid answer will probably open a floodgate of difficult questions, but because you have already established false trust, you can now lie at will. When you tell a difficult truth, the new person will believe that, if you were going to lie, you would have done so when asked the initial question.

# Build the Lie

You have decided to lie, so now you have to build your lie. Building a lie is like building an airplane. If you don't know where every single part goes and how each part works, it ain't gonna fly! Or, it might fly for a little while, but sooner or later it's going to crash.

There are two steps to building a lie:

**1.** Decide what type of lie works best in the situation.

**2.** *Know* and *remember* every detail.

## What Type of Lie Should I Tell?

There are several types of lies to tell and different situations dictate different types. The best choice, if applicable to the situation, is *Omission*.

*Lying Law #4:*
## Make Omission Your Mission

*Omission* — This is the best form of lying because you technically aren't lying at all; you are simply leaving out details that the listener doesn't need to know (and may not really want to hear).

### Example:

You're a teenage boy, and every six minutes of your day your mind is occupied with lustful thoughts. You're sitting in a living room chair across from a very large, scary, angry, protective man who was also once a sex-starved teenager, but now happens to be the middle-aged father of your date. He doesn't speak because he wants to make you uneasy and wants to see if you'll crack and just scream out, "Okay! You got me! I want to have sex with your daughter!!" He doesn't need you to scream that out. He already knows, and I guarantee you, he doesn't want to hear you say it. Oddly enough, how much he trusts you with his daughter depends on how well you lie to him.

He asks the question, "What are your intentions with my daughter?" It shouldn't take you long to *assess* that lying right now is a good idea. Instead of running scared from the house, you make omission your mission—you answer, "My intentions are to take her to dinner, then to a movie, and then have her home by midnight."

This is all true. You have simply omitted the fact that you're going to do everything in your adolescent power to have some form of sexual contact with her during that time frame.

*Deferral* — Knowing that someone else will tell the truth, so you don't have to.

**From Earlier Example:**

When Scott, your buddy, wants to ask Jennifer out

and she's out of his league, you lie to Scott and tell him he has a chance; Are you trying to embarrass Scott? No, he already thinks he has a chance (delusion) or he wouldn't have asked you. You don't need to tell him he doesn't have a chance; someone else will, and it will most likely be Jennifer. You have *deferred* the truth and doubled up pain avoidance for yourself and Scott.

*The Compliment* — Telling a lie that makes someone feel better. It's similar to deferral, except nobody is going to tell the truth to the person who asked you the initial question.

### Example:

Your wife asks you, "Honey, does my butt look big in these pants?" Of course it does, or she wouldn't have asked you that. You answer, "No, you look great." By offering her a compliment, you make her feel better and you avoid the pain of having to deal with an upset wife.

*Embellishment* — Embellishing is a high-reward, low-risk form of lying that is very different from traditional lying. You don't really care if you get "caught," because the listener probably already knows that you're making up most of it anyway. Also, you don't have to remember any of the details, because you're going to retell the same story different ways to different people. Do this whenever you can—creating stories will make you a better liar in general.

**Example:**
You go for a bike ride and nothing out of the ordinary happens. A friend asks how your ride was. You don't want to tell her that it was just a normal ride. That's boring. Tell her that you were flying down a hill when an old lady stepped off the curb, you swerved into the street to miss her, and just as you swerved, a speeding bus almost mowed you down, missing you by inches. And then tell her that her hair looks really good today. You might squeeze a nice dinner or a couple of drinks out of her.

*Pre-Emptive Strike* — If you know you're going to have to lie to someone, do it before he or she asks you the question.

**Example:**

You find out that someone at the store is going to ask you to cover their shift. You tell him any number of things ranging from "My mom is coming into town this weekend" to "I'm volunteering at the homeless shelter this weekend." He might ask you questions about your hours of volunteering or mom-time-spending, but probably not—you have already put in his mind that you are not a viable replace-ment option, and he will scurry off to find someone else to help him.

*Bumblebee* — Just as a bumblebee can only sting once and then it dies, there are certain lies that you can only tell once...or twice tops.

**Example:**

My grandma died.

*Bald-Faced* — The last resort. This is a blatant untruth.

**Example:**

You're driving home from a party. You've had a few drinks, but you're certain you're sober enough to drive safely. A police officer pulls you over and asks you if you have been drinking. The correct answer is *no*. The chances of him giving you a test are much less if you say no than if you say, "I had a couple, but I'm fine."

## Knowing and Remembering Every Detail

You have to *know and remember* every detail of your lies, but you cannot write them down. If you are thinking about keeping a "lying journal" or any other form of documentation that records your lies, think again. Artful liars never resort to recording their lies or their secrets anywhere but in the deepest recesses of their powerful, creative, lie-telling minds. If you have trouble remembering to *not* write things down, your journey to artful lying will be a long one.

**Example:**

Nixon recorded all of his phone calls.

## *Lying Law #5:*
### Don't Write Your Wrongs

Here are a couple other hard rules that will help you avoid disaster:

**1.** You cannot be in two places at the same time.

**2.** Don't include other people in your lies unless absolutely necessary. They may not have the same lying skills as you and they also cannot be in two places at the same time.

**3.** Make everything you say not only possible, but probable.

## *Convince Yourself It's True*

**"The visionary lies to himself, the liar only to others."**

**—Friedrich Nietzsche**

**"All men are frauds. The only differ-
ence between them is that some
admit it. I myself deny it."**
**—H. L. Mencken**

It is often said that if you want others to love you, you
must first love yourself. I don't know if that is true or
not, but I know this: If you want others to believe your
lies, you must first believe them yourself. You must convince yourself that everything you're saying is true.

Why?

That guilt we talked about earlier…the guilt that has
been passed down through several generations…is
the one thing that lets others know you're lying to
them. When you lie, your eyes look away, your
hands sweat, your heart races, and your feet shift.
These are not voluntary actions; they are physical
manifestations of a guilt that is so deeply embedded
in your psyche that you cannot stop them. And there
is only one way to not show guilt when you're lying
to someone: You have to lie to yourself.

## *Lying Law #6:*
### If You Believe the Lie, It's Gonna Fly

Once you have built your lie, you tell yourself over and over again that the story you built actually occurred...every last detail of it. Obviously it still won't be true, but it will be real to you, and that's all the truth you need.

*Note: I don't know if O.J. did it or not, but I do know that O.J. doesn't believe he did it.*

## Deliver the Lie

Now that you have assessed, built, and most importantly, convinced yourself that the lie you are telling is true, you are ready to deliver the lie.

Ironically, this is the moment of truth. It's the moment when the person you're lying to is going to decide if you're telling them a lie or not. The most difficult steps have already been taken and you haven't technically lied yet (except to yourself). Because you have built a solid lie and have convinced yourself it's true, delivering it should be effortless and seamless. However, there is an off chance that the person to whom you are telling the lie might doubt what you are telling them.

To minimize any suspicion, learn and obey the following rules of delivery.

## Commit

**"A lie told often becomes the truth."**
**—Lenin**

In the wise words of Pat Morita's character in *The Karate Kid*, "Walk on left side of road, okay. Walk on right side of road, okay. Walk in middle of road, squish like grape." In other words, lie or don't. If you lie and you think someone doubts what you say, stick to your lie. Your unwavering conviction will turn their doubt in you into self-doubt.

**Example:**

You just get home from work and all you want to do is relax. You were supposed to meet a friend for a drink, but you really don't want to go. You call him and say, "Steve, sorry, but I can't meet you tonight. I have a report I have to finish by tomorrow morning—maybe some other time." Steve is pretty shrewd. He replies, "You don't have a report due tomorrow; you just don't want to meet me." You could bail out and tell the truth now, but then Steve would know you're a liar and you would most likely get wrangled into meeting him. You commit. You state assertively, "Yes, I do have a report to write." That's it. No explanation and no story, just the same lie you originally told. If he continues and asks questions about the report, take the offensive and make him feel guilty for questioning your integrity.

## Take the D out of Your Tales

Because you have effectively built your lie, you know all the details. However, don't offer any of them to the listener. The instant you offer details, you not only sound like you're lying, but you open the door for questions about those details. Inevitably, you end up *stacking* your lies (i.e. "stacking" lie upon lie until they become difficult to manage and remember). If someone asks you a question regarding details, your preparation will pay off. You will confidently and quickly offer only necessary specifics, allaying any suspicion your listener might have with an air of apparent honesty.

**Example:**
In the previous example, you tell Steve you have a report—that's it. Do you know what type of report? How many pages? Who's going to see it? Of course, but don't tell Steve. It's none of his business.

*Lying Law #7:*
*Know Details, but No Details*

## No "Honesty," "Truth," "Belief," or "Trust"

"Honesty" is a song by Billy Joel. Let's keep it that way. When lying, don't qualify what you're saying by using any form of words such as truth, belief, trust, or honesty. "To tell you the truth," "To be honest with you," "Believe me...," "Trust me...," etc., are tell-tale signs that you are either lying right now or that you are telling the truth right now, but you lie most of the time.

**Example:**
You take your car to a mechanic because the car is making some sounds that it wasn't making yesterday. The mechanic listens to it, tilts his head in thought, and says, "To tell you the truth, it sounds like your [insert expensive car part here]." He's lying. Trust me, I mean no offense to any mechanics who are reading this...honest.

## *Lying Law #8:*
### Qualifying Equals Lying

### Watch Your "But"

Avoid the use of the word "but" when lying. This is not a hard rule, but more of something to be mindful of. Just pay attention to when other people use "but" when they're talking to you. You'll notice how most of the time, everything they say before "but" is a lie.

**Example:**
You're in a carpool with Mary and Joe. You drop Joe off at his house. As you pull away, Mary says, "I really like Joe, but I think he likes himself more." Mary doesn't like Joe. She thinks he's an egomaniacal &#$!face.

*Escape the Situation*

**"People don't like to be lied to. They want you to get away with it."**
**—Tino Lucente**

Once you have delivered the lie, there is no reason to hang around. If you have to hang around (e.g., you are at a meeting and have to lie during the meeting), wait until the last possible moment to deliver your lie, leaving yourself less time between the delivery and your escape moment.

If someone tries to corner you, quickly build a new lie regarding why you have to leave right now.

*Lying Law #9:*
*Tell One, Be Done, Then Run*

# Chapter 7

## Exceptions to the Rules

"**Nothing is easier than self-deceit. For what each man wishes, that he also believes to be true.**"

**—Demosthenes**

There are two situations when you do not completely follow the ABCDE's of Lying: calling in sick and breaking up with someone. You would have inevitably figured out these two exceptions to the rules on your own, but I wanted to save you the time and energy.

# Calling in Sick

**Assessing:**

Should I lie to my boss and play golf with my brother?

Yes.

**Building**:

What type of lie am I going to tell?

Omission...of course. How? There is not a kernel of truth about you being sick. Not true. Here is the lie: "I'm not coming in today. I'm sick." You omit, "...of coming into work."

It's time for the details. Know how long you have been sick, what kind of sick you were, what time you started feeling bad, when your fever broke, what movies you halfway-watched on TBS when you were in and out of consciousness, who brought you Sprite and crackers, etc. Manufacture every detail of the story and then...*don't convince yourself it's true.*

This is the exception to the rule. You cannot convince yourself that you are really sick or your body will play psychosomatic tricks on you and you will actually become ill, defeating the purpose of calling in sick in the first place.

**Delivering:**

When calling in sick to work, *don't sound sick.* I know this sounds preposterous, but most of us have never taken an acting class. The dead giveaway that you're lying is when you moan, groan, or speak in a whispery, but husky, voice. And whatever you do, don't cough. *Coughing equals lying.*

Simply call from a horizontal position and speak normally. If the party from the night before is still going on, call from a different room...or house.

Most importantly (and this is the case with any lie, except embellishment), *do not offer extraneous details.*

**Bad example (raspy sick voice):**

My throat kind of had that tickly feeling in the back

of it when I went to bed last night, and when I woke up at like 2:30 this morning, I could barely swallow. Now my head hurts and I'm achy and whatever it is that started in my throat is working its way into my lungs (fake cough here).

**Good example (normal voice):**
I'm not coming to work today. I'm sick.

Your boss will rarely ask you what's wrong. If he does, he's testing you to see if you will break into some detail-laden lie. So if he asks, always tell him as succinctly as possible that it's a stomach thing. This goes back to the voice. When you have a sick stomach, you can still speak, and no one wants to hear about how many times you had to rush to the toilet in the last six hours.

**Escaping:**
In this instance, escaping quickly is a win-win. You want to get off the phone before you have to answer any questions, and the sooner you get off the phone, the sicker your boss thinks you are.

Nobody who feels like they're going to puke wants to make small talk.

Last, but not least, when calling in sick: You have to be sick at least two days in a row. *Length of illness validates illness.*

# Breaking Up with Someone

When breaking up with someone, you should go no further in the lying process than assessing whether or not to lie, because your answer should be, "No, don't lie." You probably believe that you will save their feelings if you lie. You also probably believe that you will avoid pain if you lie. Let's face it, when you break up with someone, they are going to make you feel pain whether you tell them the truth or not.

Building and Convincing and Delivering would not be too different from any other lie, but Escape from this situation is *impossible*. He or she will grill you relentlessly, asking every agonizing question in the book, until you become so frustrated and annoyed that you will undoubtedly tell them the truth, so you might as well just tell them the truth from the outset.

I recommend the following true, but brutal, phrase (or a reasonable facsimile):

*"It's not you, it's me…not liking you anymore."*

# Chapter 8

## Knowing When Someone Is Lying to You

**"People who whisper lie."**

**—Swedish Proverb**

I don't need to tell you how to know someone is lying to you, because at this point, you are well on your way to becoming an artful liar. However, here's a little recap. Watch for:

*The physiological guilt signs*: Looking in another direction after speaking, sweaty palms, shifting of the feet, etc.

*The key words:* Anything relating to truth, honesty, belief, or trust—and, of course, "but."

*Details:* When someone is telling the truth, they don't have to make up a story. A "story" signals a lie.

If you're still not sure if someone is lying to you or not, corner him, make him stack, make him squirm. It'll be fun...for you.

Note: If someone is embellishing, and you know they're making up crap, enjoy the story, tell them you know they're lying, and thank them for not wasting your time with a boring story.

# Conclusion

> "They say that in the end truth will triumph, but it's a lie."
> —Anton Pavlovich Chekhov

This book is ending, but your journey is just beginning. If you are still reading, and you didn't skip over the parts in the middle, you are on the path to being an artful liar.

Let's recap the lying laws:

### *Lying Law #1*
*The Truth Hurts, but I Don't*

### *Lying Law #2*
*Life's More Fun When Tales Are Spun*

*Lying Law #3*
If You Lie to Succeed,
You Succeed in Lying

*Lying Law #4*
Make Omission Your Mission

*Lying Law #5*
Don't Write Your Wrongs

*Lying Law #6*
If You Believe the Lie, It's Gonna Fly

*Lying Law #7*
Know Details, but No Details

*Lying Law #8*
Qualifying Equals Lying

*Lying Law #9*
Tell One, Be Done, Then Run

If you follow these lying laws, believe in yourself, believe your own lies, and follow the ABCDE's (adding your personal flair and style of course), you will have a long and fruitful lying career. Please be mindful that with great lying power comes great responsibility. So before I send you off on your own, I want to leave you with one thought: People don't like to be lied to, so you owe it to them to remember the most important Lying Law of all:

*Lying Law #10 — The Golden Rule*
*Don't get caught.*

# About the Author

Duke is not his real name.